Go Wild

BE A
TRACKER

Thanks to the creative team:
Senior Editor: Alice Peebles
Designer: Lauren Woods and collaborate agency

Hungry Tomato™
A division of Lerner Publishing Group, Inc.
241 First Avenue North
Minneapolis, MN 55401 USA

For reading levels and more information, look up this title
at www.lernerbooks.com.

Main body text set in Zemke Hand ITC 14/1.7
Typeface provided by International Typeface Corporation

Library of Congress Cataloging-in-Publication Data

Oxlade, Chris.
    Be a tracker / Chris Oxlade, Eva Sassin.
        pages cm. — (Go wild)
    "Original Edition Copyright © 2016 Hungry Tomato Ltd."
    Audience: Ages 8–12
    Audience: Grades 4 to 6
    ISBN 978-1-4677-6359-2 (lb : alk. paper)
    ISBN 978-1-4677-7650-9 (pb : alk. paper)
    ISBN 978-1-4677-7225-9 (eb pdf)
    1. Tracking and trailing—Juvenile literature. 2. Animal
tracks—Juvenile literature. 3. Animal behavior—Juvenile
literature. I. Sassin, Eva, author. II. Title.
    SK282.O95 2016
    591.47'9—dc23   2015007522

Manufactured in the United States of America
1 - VP - 7/15/15

Go Wild BE A TRACKER

By Chris Oxlade

Illustrated by Eva Sassin

HUNGRY TOMATO™

Minneapolis

CONTENTS

TIME TO GO WILD

Where do you go to have fun? Have you tried exploring the great outdoors? No? Then it's time to go wild! Out in the wild, you can track animals, explore ponds and rivers, and have a load of fun. Even if you live in the middle of a city, you can have a wild time in your backyard, your local park, or another place where you have an adult's permission to explore and where it's safe and legal to do so.

Step outdoors to discover some of the skills needed to carefully follow animal tracks, stay hidden while watching animals, and catch and study all sorts of fascinating creepy crawlies.

WILD SAFETY

- Always ask an adult before going tracking in the wild. In particular, ask before going near or in water.
- Ask an adult before you do any of the projects in this book.
- Beware of dangerous or poisonous wild animals.
- Always wash your hands after handling bugs or soil.

CARING FOR THE ENVIRONMENT

Always take care of the environment when you are in the wild. That means:

- Never damage rocks, animals, or plants.
- Take special care to keep fires under control. Make sure a fire is out before you leave it.

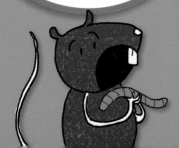

FOLLOW THE TRACKS

ANIMAL TRACKING SKILLS

To watch animals in the wild, you first have to find them—and that means recognizing their tracks. Tracking skills will help you to follow animals by looking for footprints, paw prints and hoof prints, and other signs left by animals.

Looking for tracks

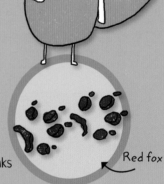

Red fox

1. The best places to search for animal tracks are muddy paths, the muddy banks of rivers, and beaches. Tracks will be clearer when the ground is damp, early in the morning, or in the evening, when the sun is low in the sky. Walk slowly, looking carefully at the ground.

A deer track in mud

2. Try to match the tracks you find to the diagrams on this page. See if you can learn some common animal prints.

Rabbit

Cat

Gray squirrel

Deer

Dog

Black bear

It's a good idea to put a tape measure next to prints when you photograph them.

3. In winter, tracks are easy to see in fresh snow.

4. Try taking photographs of the tracks you find. Use the close-up setting on your camera. Photograph from a low position and at an angle, to make them more visible. Take photographs of lines of prints as well as single prints.

5. If you find a trail of prints, see how far you can follow them—they might lead you to an animal's home.

Detective rat

Studying bird tracks

Sandy beaches and muddy riverbanks are good places to find bird tracks. Beware of sinking in soft mud on riverbanks, though.

Chicken

Pigeon

Blackbird

Duck

Eagle

Crow

Sparrow

At the beach, look for tracks after the tide goes out. At the riverbank, look after the river level has fallen. Try to match any bird tracks you find to these diagrams.

Making Molds

You can make copies of animal tracks in three dimensions. You'll need some plaster of Paris from an art supply store.

1. Put a cardboard ring (such as the inside from a roll of duct tape) around the print.

2. Mix a small amount of plaster of Paris, following the instructions on the packet. Carefully pour the plaster of Paris into the ring.

3. Allow the plaster of Paris to dry for about fifteen minutes, then carefully dig up the ring, taking a layer of soil with the plaster.

4. Take the ring home and leave it for a few hours as it hardens. Then remove the ring and clean the dirt off the plaster.

5. Label your mold to show when and where you found the print, and what animal you think might have made the track.

Excuse me! Fox coming through!

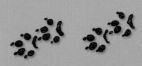

More signs for tracking

Animals leave other clues besides their footprints.

As you search for tracks, keep an eye out for nibbled bits of food and pieces of fur.

A pine cone eaten by a squirrel

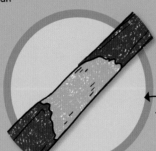

Tree bark stripped by a deer

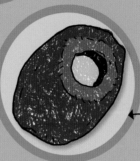

An acorn opened by a mouse

Poo clues

You can also identify animals by the droppings (poo) they leave.

Keep an eye out for droppings on the ground. Try to match them to the references here. Don't touch the droppings!

Deer droppings

Fox droppings

Rabbit droppings

Angry squirrel with poo on his foot!

FOLLOW THE LEADER

MAKING AND FOLLOWING TRAILS

You can have fun laying trails in the wild for your friends to follow. Try playing games where you creep up on your friends. These activities will be good practice for your tracking skills.

Laying a trail

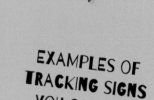

1. Organize yourself and your friends into two teams—runners and trackers. The runners take off first, laying a trail as they go. Each time they reach a junction or change direction, they leave a sign to show which way they have gone. You can do this with sticks, stones, leaves, or flour.

2. The trackers wait a couple of minutes and then try to follow the signs. Can they catch the runners?

EXAMPLES OF TRACKING SIGNS YOU CAN USE

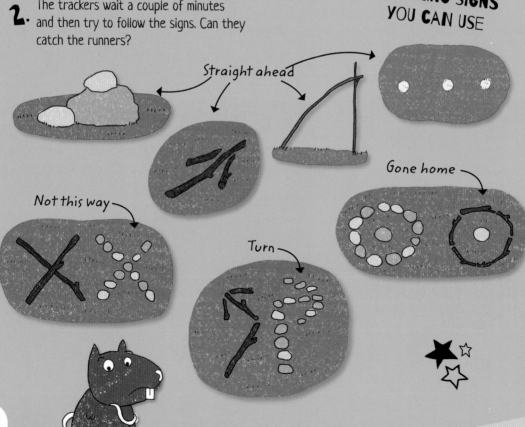

Straight ahead

Not this way

Turn

Gone home

Hunter and prey game

In this game, you (the hunter) try to creep up on a friend (the prey). Your friend has a water pistol and will soak you if he or she hears you. The game will help you to practice moving quietly in the wild—and, if you are the one with the water pistol, to listen really carefully.

1. Choose a person to be the prey. He or she must stand in one place, holding a filled water pistol and wearing a blindfold. The hunters must move about 165 feet (50 meters) away. When everyone is ready, the hunters must try to creep silently up to the prey and touch him or her before being heard.

2. If the prey hears a noise, he or she can fire the water pistol—aiming at where the noise came from—to try and soak the hunter.

Oops! These two have the game all wrong!

HIDE IN THE WILD

MAKING CAMOUFLAGE

When you are tracking small animals or watching birds, it's best not to let the animals or birds spot you. Otherwise, they will get nervous and run or fly away. By wearing camouflage, you can easily blend in with the undergrowth. Or use camouflage to hide from your friends!

Camouflage face paint

2. Apply the paints to your face, in front of a mirror if possible. Use patches of color to break up the shape of your face.

3. In an emergency, you can use mud or charcoal scraped from burned sticks for face camouflage.

1. You can use store-bought face paints for this. Choose dark colors such as greens, browns, and blacks. Or make your own face paint. Mix skin lotion, cornflour, and food coloring. Start with some lotion. Mix the coloring in slowly and then add cornflour to thicken it.

A camouflage shirt

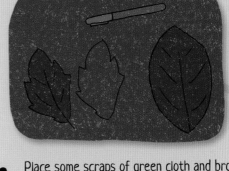

2. Place some scraps of green cloth and brown cloth on a table. Lay your leaves on the cloth and draw around them with a marker pen. Draw about 30 leaf shapes. Cut out the leaves.

1. Collect some large leaves. The project works best if you use green leaves that have just fallen to the ground.

3. Glue your cut-out leaves to a dark-brown or dark-green T-shirt with fabric glue, overlapping them to cover most of the shirt.

A camouflage hat

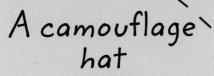

1. Find a dark-colored baseball cap or knit hat. Gather some twigs and small leafy branches. Attach them to the hat with sticky tape or safety pins.

Camouflage skunk!

13

SPOT THE FLYERS

BIRD AND BAT WATCHING

By building a bird hide and a bird box, you can get close to birds in the wild. That way, you can study them and perhaps spot some birds you have never seen before.

Oh, if only I could find a home!

Make a bird hide

Set up this bird hide in a wooded area or on the shore of a lake, where there are plenty of birds.

2. Lean branches against the crossbar to make a screen. Leave a space to look through the center of the screen. Sit behind the screen and watch for birds. Use binoculars to view them more clearly.

1. Make two A-frames about 3 feet (1 m) high by lashing together two pairs of sticks about 5 feet (1.5 m) long. Lay a crossbar between them and tie the crossbar in place.

Hoot, hoot!

Make a nesting box

A nesting box will attract small birds looking for a place to nest.

Front	Back	Side	Side	Base	Lid
8 in (20 cm)	16 in (40 cm)	10 in (25 cm)	8 in (20 cm)		10 in (25 cm)

6 in (15 cm)

1 in (25 mm) hole

4.7 in (12 cm)

1. With an adult's help, cut out shapes from a plank of wood, 6 inches (15 cm) wide and about 0.5 inches (1.5 cm) thick, as shown in the diagram.

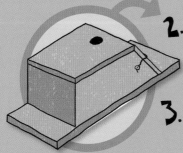

2. Glue the parts together. For the moment, leave off the lid.

3. Glue a small block of wood inside the lid to stop it sliding off. Also put a small screw in each side of the box and the lid. Tie a string to the screws to keep the lid on.

I wonder who lives here . . .

4. Ask an adult to help you nail your box on a tree, at least six feet (1.8 m) off the ground.

Looking for bats

Look for bats at dusk, when they emerge from their nests to hunt insects. Take an adult with you. Woodlands and alongside rivers are good places to look. So is the night sky in cities.

1. Stand still and look up towards the sky and listen. Watch for small black shapes flying low and listen for high-pitched squeaks.

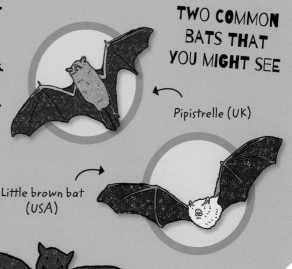

Pipistrelle (UK)

Little brown bat (USA)

Hi, guys!

DOWN BY THE WATER

EXPLORING PONDS AND RIVERS

You can find all sorts of creatures by exploring your local pond or stream. They live on the pond or riverbed, in the water, and on the surface. All you need is a simple net to find them.

SAFETY NEAR WATER

Always take an adult with you when exploring near water. Be careful not to slip into the water on pond edges and riverbanks.

Pond dipping

1. Start by looking above the surface of a pond or river for dragonflies, mosquitoes, and other flying insects. Then search the surface itself for animals such as whirligig beetles and water bugs.

2. Dip a net into the water. Move it slowly through the water and lift it out. Examine the net for animals. Try dipping at different depths and through the mud at the bottom of the water.

COMMON ANIMALS ABOVE AND AT THE WATER SURFACE

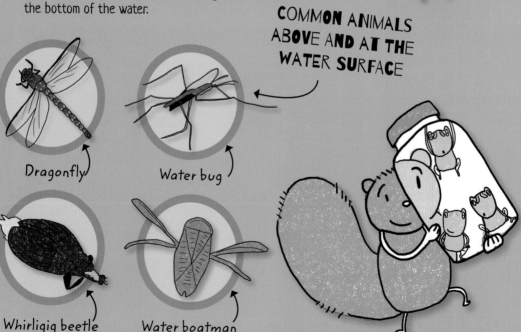

Dragonfly

Water bug

Whirligig beetle

Water boatman

3. Put your captured animals into a clean jam jar or a plastic jug with some pond water inside. Examine them with a magnifying glass. Release them before going home.

Pond snail

Fresh-water shrimps

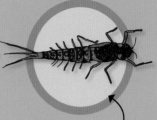

Mayfly nymph

Sssso many pond animals to sssspot!

Stickleback

Newt

Looking after tadpoles

Try watching frogs eggs grow into tadpoles. First, get an adult's help to check the laws in your area.

2. When the tadploes begin to hatch, add a little fish food to the water.

3. After a few weeks, your tadpoles will start growing legs. This is the time to release them back to the pond, if it's legal in your area.

1. If it's legal where you live, collect frog spawn in the spring by dipping a jar into a pond. Only take a small amount. You can also get these eggs at a pet store. At home, put the frogspawn into a plastic tub with some water. Add a few stones in the bottom of the tub.

BUG BUSINESS

HUNTING AND CATCHING CREEPY CRAWLIES

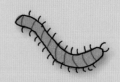

The wild is full of bugs. Millions of them! They might not be as easy to see as larger animals and birds, but you can find them if you know where to look. Then you can catch and keep them.

Bug dinner

Put out tasty treats to attract some bugs to watch.

1. Make a sticky mixture of old mashed banana and sugar. Then smear a little of it on a stick. Leave the stick outdoors, under a bush or stone. Return the next day to see what creatures have been attracted. You can also look at night with a flashlight.

2. If you want to study a bug more closely, carefully place it into a clear container with a lid and air holes. You can look at it with a magnifying glass.

COMMON CREATURES YOU MIGHT SEE

Did you see any of these common garden bugs?

Garden snail

Slug

Roly-poly bug

Ground beetle

Harvestman

I know I'm not a snail, but can I be your friend too?

Dead log safari

Rotting logs from dead trees are teeming with bugs! They feed off the rotting wood and off other bugs and plants that live there.

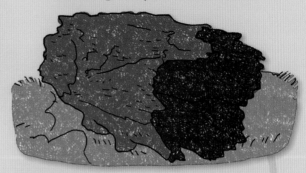

1. First, find a rotting log (this will probably be in a forest). Examine the top and sides of the log. Pull off pieces of rotting wood to look underneath. Use a magnifying glass to study any bugs you find.

2. Lift away dead leaves and twigs to see under the log, but always put them back afterwards.

BUGS YOU MIGHT FIND IN A DEAD LOG.

Black ant

Millipede

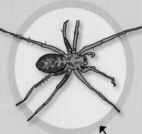

House spider

Snail friends

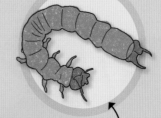

beetle larva

Pitfall trap for bugs

Try setting up this simple trap to catch bugs that are exploring your backyard during the night.

1. Take a large, clean jar to your bug-catching site (the woods or your backyard). Dig a hole just big enough for the jar to fit into, so the neck of the jar is level with the ground.

2. Put a small piece of cheese in the jar to attract bugs. Place three small stones on the ground around the jar. Lay a flat rock, a brick, or an old tile on top. There should be a small gap between the stones and the rim of the jar.

3. Leave the trap to do its work overnight. What bugs did you catch?

BUGS YOU MIGHT FIND IN YOUR TRAP

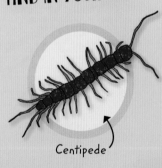

Centipede

Beetle

Earwig

This trap is meant for bugs! Not for rodents!

A bug hotel

Here's how to build a fancy hotel where bugs will come and live. Well, fancy for bugs!

Can birds stay here too?

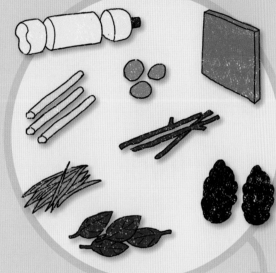

1. Find an old wooden drawer or wooden box, about 1.6 by 0.9 feet (50 by 30 cm).

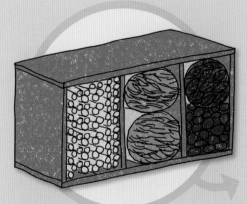

2. To divide the box into sections, add cardboard sheets cut to size and sleeves made of plastic bottles. Make short bamboo sticks, break up twigs, add bundles of leaves, and find some stones.

3. Install your materials in the box to complete the bug hotel.

4. Leave your bug hotel in the garden and check every day to see what's moved in . . .

It's vacation time for the bug family!

WATCH THOSE WORMS

MAKING A WORMERY

Soil is full of worms! You can catch some of these fascinating creatures and make a wormery (a special home) for them. Then you can watch them at work in the soil.

EARTHWORM FACTS

• Wriggling earthworms burrow through the soil and eat rotting leaves and vegetation.

• They help plants to grow by breaking up the soil and mixing air into it.

• There are around 6,000 different types of earthworm.

• Earthworms are male and female at the same time.

Build a wormery

Ask an adult to help you with this project.

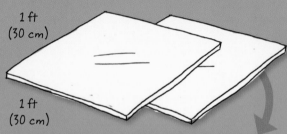

1 ft (30 cm)

1 ft (30 cm)

1. You need two sheets of stiff clear plastic (called acrylic), both about 4.6 square inches (30 sq. cm). Find an old wooden drawer or wooden box, about 1.5 ft by 1 ft (50 by 30 cm).

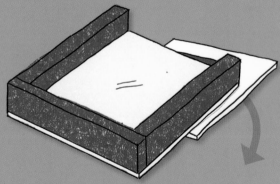

2. Next you need some strips of wood about 1 in (3 cm) thick. Put one of your sheets of plastic on a counter. Then cut strips of wood to fit along three sides of the plastic, as shown. Glue the pieces on with waterproof glue.

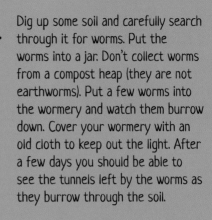

5. Dig up some soil and carefully search through it for worms. Put the worms into a jar. Don't collect worms from a compost heap (they are not earthworms). Put a few worms into the wormery and watch them burrow down. Cover your wormery with an old cloth to keep out the light. After a few days you should be able to see the tunnels left by the worms as they burrow through the soil.

3. Glue the second plastic sheet on top of the strips of wood. Wait for the glue to dry completely.

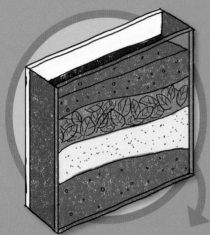

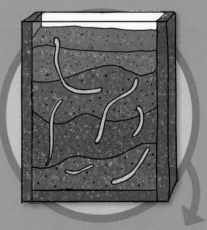

6. Gradually the worms will mix up the layers of mold, soil, and sand. If the top layer is beginning to dry out, add a little more water.

4. Collect some leaf mold, some sand, and some soil. Put layers of mold, sand, and soil into the wormery, one on top of the other. Add a little water to keep the layers damp.

7. You can also make a simple wormery in a large plastic bottle.

Try not to eat the worms . . .

23

SNAIL SAFARI

KEEPING AND RACING SNAILS

Snails are easy to find in the wild. Before you start looking, make sure you know the rules about raising snails in your area. Then find out how to collect and keep them in a snail farm, as well as how to hold a snail race.

Safari bat!

Start a snail farm

Ask an adult to help you with this project.

1. Find a container for your snails, such as an old, clear plastic box. Drill or puncture some holes in the lid to let fresh air get in. Put plenty of food in the container for your snails: a mixture of leaves from different plants and chopped up old fruit works well.

2. Now find some snails from the wild or your garden. Search under leaves and rocks. Then put the snails you find in a plastic box. At home, carefully put the snails into your snail farm. Put the farm in a cool place out of direct sunlight to stop it from drying out.

3. Watch the snails over the next few days. Number some small stickers. Then stick them carefully on the different snails to identify them.

4. Return all your snails to the wild after a few days.

Hold a snail race

Try holding a race with the snails from your farm!

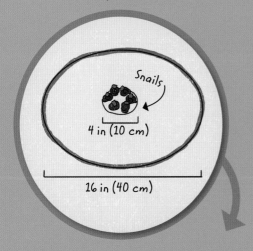

Snails

4 in (10 cm)

16 in (40 cm)

What's this I hear about a safari?

1. Prepare a race arena by drawing two circles on a large piece of card, one about 4 inches (10 cm) across, and one about 16 inches (40 cm) across (draw around pan lids or bowls to make the circles).

2. Mark your snails with stickers (see left) so you can identify the winner. Put all the snails in the center ring and release them. First snail to cross the outside line wins the race!

Snails (and a beaver) on safari!

SNAIL FACTS AND FIGURES

- Snails live on land, in lakes and rivers, and in the sea.

- The giant tiger land snail grows up to a foot (30 cm) long.

- Snail shells are made from calcium carbonate.

- A snail has thousands of microscopic teeth.

WINGS AND WEBS

CATCHING MOTHS AND SPIDER'S WEBS

Dozens of different types of moth flit about during the night, when you are asleep. You can catch them quite easily to study them. The mornings are a good time to look for spider's webs, which you can collect and keep.

Catching moths at night

Ask an adult to help you with this project.

1. Hang an old white sheet outdoors so that it hangs vertically, like a wall. Set up a bright light, such as a camping lamp or bright flashlight, to light up the sheet. Wait until nighttime.

2. When it's dark, moths should be attracted to the light and land on the sheet. Examine them with a magnifying glass and photograph them if you like.

26

Collecting spider's webs

1. First, find a spider's web. If a spider is in the middle of the web, blow gently and it should crawl off. If it stays put, look for another web. Take a handful of talcum powder in your palm and blow across it so that the powder blows onto the web.

2. Spray a thick sheet of black paper with hair spray. Put the sheet behind the web and slowly move it forward until it touches the web.

3. Remove any threads at the edges of the card. Then remove the card.

4. You can make your web picture permanent with artist's fixing spray.

SPIDER'S WEB FACTS

Spider's webs are incredible feats of engineering!

• The webs you are looking for in this project are called orb webs and are made by orb-web spiders.

• Spider-web silk is as strong as steel when stretched.

• Spiders use sticky and non-sticky threads to make their webs.

DON'T GET EATEN!

AVOIDING DANGEROUS ANIMALS

It's great fun to track and watch animals in the wild, but there are some animals you should never get too close to. They could attack you if they're hungry or defending themselves. Some are dangerous because they are big. Some have poisonous bites.

SNAKES AND SPIDERS

If you are tracking somewhere where poisonous snakes and spiders live, make sure you don't accidentally step on one. When looking for bugs, turn over logs and stones with a stick, not with your hands. Also check your clothes and shoes for snakes and spiders before getting dressed.

Avoid insect bites

Bites from mosquitoes and other insects are unpleasant and can be dangerous. Steer clear of stagnant water, where mosquitoes live. Keep your skin covered, especially at night. Wear long pants and long sleeves. Use a mosquito net (or cover up with a head scarf and glasses, (*above*). Don't worry about looking silly!

A mosquito—one to avoid!

Beware of bears

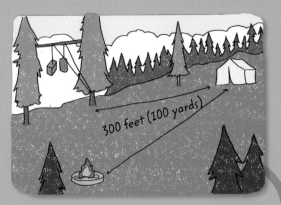

300 feet (100 yards)

The black bear is the most common bear in North America.

1. Bears enjoy food! So when you are camping in bear country, put your food in bear-proof boxes, at least 164 feet (50 m) from your tent, or in an airtight container hanging from a pole or branch in a tree. Never leave food in your tent! Do your cooking well away from your tent and keep your camp clear of smelly garbage.

2. Make plenty of noise when you are moving around, so you don't surprise a bear. Stay away from dead animals, which could be their food. If you see a bear in the distance, don't go any closer—especially if it's with its young or feeding.

3. If you are unfortunate enough to come face to face with a bear, stay calm and quiet, and don't look it in the eye. Back away with your head lowered. Never turn and run or climb a tree to escape—bears are better runners and climbers than humans!

4. If a bear catches you, play dead.

29

DID YOU KNOW?

○ In some places in the world, you can see fossilized dinosaur tracks from millions of years ago. But you won't track down a dinosaur by following them!

○ The biggest dinosaur footprints found measure 5 feet (1.5 m) across—that's three times as wide as an elephant's footprint. The dinosaur that made the prints must have been 82 feet (25 m) long.

○ In 1951 giant footprints were found in the snow of the Himalayas. They were not bear prints. Many people believe they were made by an apelike creature known as a yeti, which nobody has ever seen.

○ Do you think you have a good sense of smell for tracking? You might have, but you're not as good as a bloodhound. They have a sense of smell that is a thousand times more sensitive than humans'. They can sniff out the scent of humans many days after the people have gone.

○ Many Aboriginal people in Australia are skilled trackers. An experienced Aboriginal tracker can tell the size, weight, age, and gender of an animal from its tracks.

○ People often use the phrase 'snail's pace' to mean moving slowly. But what is a snail's pace? It's about 164 feet (50 m) per hour.

These snails are moving at a snail's pace.

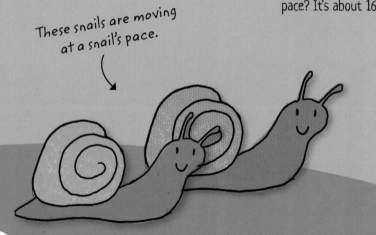

Hurry up! You two are so slow!

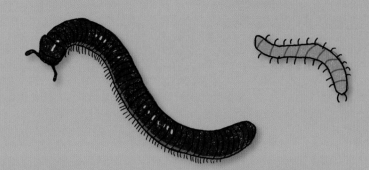

○ If you catch a centipede, try counting its legs. Centipedes don't have a hundred legs, as you might think. They normally have between 30 and 354 legs.

○ The world's biggest bat is the Australian flying fox, which has a wingspan of more than 3 feet (1 m).

○ A typical frog lays about 20,000 eggs in a pond. The eggs develop into tadpoles, but only one tadpole in 1,000 survives to grow into a frog.

○ In healthy soil, there will be about 250 earthworms per 35 cubic feet (1 cubic meter).

○ Some people think bears can't run downhill. They can – at about 40 miles (60 kilometers) per hour. That's twice as fast as you can run!

○ The world biggest moth is the colorful Atlas moth from Southeast Asia. Its wingspan is a foot (30 cm). Atlas moth caterpillars grow more than 4 inches (10 cm) long.

○ Darwin's bark spider, which lives in Madagascar, weaves a web up to 82 feet (25 m) across!

So many babies!

INDEX

THE AUTHOR
Chris Oxlade is an experienced author of educational books for children. He has written more than two hundred books on science, technology, sports and hobbies, including many activity and project books. He enjoys camping and adventurous outdoor sports including rock climbing, hill running, kayaking and sailing. He lives in England with his wife, children, and dogs.

THE ARTIST
Eva Sassin is a freelance illustrator born and bred in London, England. She has loved illustrating ever since she can remember, and she loves combining characters with unusual textures to give them more depth and keep them interesting.